Swim Fit Swimming
Swimming For Fitness And Health

Published By Shaharm Publications

SHAHARM PUBLICATIONS

For a full list of books by Shaharm Publications, please go to:

http://www.shaharmpublications.com

Table of Contents

Introduction

Water: It fuels the body, allows life to exist, and is a useful tool for health and fitness. Most people are aware of the health benefits of drinking water. Drinking water prior, during, and after exercise makes it a useful tool for fitness. However, swimming gives humans a new way to use water to improve their lives.

Swimming is nothing new. Cave paintings found in Egypt are believed to depict ancient people swimming, and these paintings are more than 10,000 years old. However, the realization of swimming as a way to improve health and fitness may not have been discovered until the 1600's, when it finally took the spotlight in the scientific community.

Over the course of the centuries, swimming has evolved quite a bit, primarily as a competitive sport. Swimmers are constantly discovering or inventing new techniques for swimming faster, more effectively, or while wasting less energy. That's the beauty of swimming: it's incredibly versatile and suitable for many different situations, including health and fitness. More on the history of swimming will be covered in depth in the next chapter.

Today, people all over the world swim to get fit, reduce symptoms from serious illnesses and to improve mental health. You don't need to be a professional swimmer or an Olympic athlete to get into the water and enjoy the many benefits of swimming. All of the benefits of swimming will be covered in later chapters.

A Brief History of Swimming

The Internet is full of miracle drugs, overnight programs, and fitness regimes that claim to work magic on the body. Once a person has spent enough time having their hopes crushed time and time again with these false claims, being skeptical becomes second nature. It becomes easier to dismiss swimming as another "fitness miracle", than to recognize the many merits it possesses.

However, swimming has something that none of these other fitness programs has: a long history. Swimming has been around for thousands of years. It isn't something a couple of young guys thought up during a brainstorming session. It isn't something that's going to be sold on the web. As a matter of fact, it doesn't even cost a dime if you can find a free place to swim.

Swimming has a history, and understanding that history makes it easier to believe that swimming can be used to do many great things, such as improve mental health, and even build muscle mass.

The history of swimming is really a history of the entire world. Its first days, however, are unknown. Several prehistoric paintings found on cave walls and pottery suggests that even ancient people understood the basic principles of swimming. This place became known as "The Cave of Swimmers".

Whether these ancient paintings truly depict variations of the front crawl or breaststroke - different swimming techniques - or are just paintings of ritual acts, is a subject of much debate. The world may never know if the caveman in these particular paintings were actually swimming, but there is much more certainty in later depictions.

The written history of swimming came some time later. It was mentioned in places throughout the Bible, the Odyssey, and Beowulf. Ancient civilizations, such as the Romans and the Greeks, were avid swimmers and seriously competitive. These were some of the toughest men and soldiers the world had ever seen, the same men who created the original Olympic Games. Oddly enough, swimming was not yet a part of the Olympic Games during these early years.

The Greeks took the time to build small swimming pools in their bath areas. Greeks would often insult one another by claiming the other could neither run nor swim. Philosophers of the time believed not being able to swim was a sign of a lack of a proper education.

Records from a later time indicate that the Japanese were also very fond of swimming. It was implemented as a regular part of their military training. Other writings show records of regularly held swimming competitions.

What's more is that many high-ranking generals promoted swimming during this time for its many health and fitness benefits. Already, during the 8th century, people realized that swimming was a healthy activity and it was highly recommended.

Charlemagne often preached about the benefits of swimming to those who met him and his family alike. Those who knew Charlemagne would say that he was an extremely strong swimmer and one of the best at the sport. At this time, young boys and men often did swimming as a leisure activity. Any time boys gathered to swim, swimming races eventually took place.

Children raised in monasteries were also given some leisure time to swim, because they believed it had many positive impacts on the human body and mind. Through time, many beliefs of these days would be found wrong, but the benefits of swimming still stand true.

Swimming would slowly decline in popularity. This was due largely to the growing conservative nature of civilization throughout the 16th century. It eventually became illegal in Germany for children to swim naked in public areas.

In 1538, the first book dedicated entirely to swimming was published. It was entitled "Colyembetes". However, this book was not written to educate readers on the many benefits of swimming, instead, it was drafted with the purpose of reducing the number of people who drown because they simply couldn't swim.

The book was widely regarded as a definitive guide to learning to swim, especially when nothing else like it existed at the time. It taught readers an effective method for learning breaststroke, as well as outlining proper safety techniques and the use of possible floatation devices, such as a cork belt.

Cork belts were used at the time as temporary floatation devices. Unfortunately, the corks would eventually rot or become waterlogged. If this happened, and the person couldn't swim, then they faced serious danger.

Shortly afterwards, another book about swimming was written in England by E. Digby. This book became well known because it claimed humans had the potential to swim better than the fish, a creature that lives its entire life swimming in the water.

The next century would lead to the rise of the first national swimming organization, which was located in Japan. During this time, emperor Yozei declared that swimming should be part of the education process for all children.

Swimming even became one of the necessary arts of the samurai. Suiejutsu is the martial art of swimming, which translates into "water art". Samurais were specially trained to swim while wearing their gear. Swimming was also implemented because ruling parties realized the significant impact it had on the body of the swimmers.

Barely more than a decade later, Queen Anne would bring swimming and the health impacts of water back into the spotlight. She stated that a recent visit to a bath spa had increased her well being. This brought a lot of attention to something that was slowly dying away.

The Prince of Wales would introduce his father to the health benefits of swimming in the sea during the 18th century. This caused a massive boost in the popularity of swimming, particularly in salt waters. Markets began selling miracle drugs and tonics that claimed to use sea salts, sea air, or water from the sea itself.

People from all over Europe began to view swimming and bathing as a health-conscious act. It was extremely popular amongst people with wealth, and high-ranking visitors from other countries. During this time, the increase in popularity caused more attention to once again turn to swimming as a competitive sport.

There were plenty of other significant advancements during the 18th century. In 1796, a swimming club was created in Sweden. That swimming club is still in existence to this date.

This is also the time when Benjamin Franklin, at the age of ten, invented the swimming fin.

Another famous book was written in Germany during this time. The English translation of the book is "Exercise for Youth". A large portion of the book was dedicated to swimming and its use as a low-impact form of exercise. Other books during this century covered new swimming techniques, as well as new techniques for learning to swim.

This is when the modern method for learning to swim was first designed. It is a simple three stage process that includes getting comfortable with the water, learning individual moves for swimming outside of the water, and then applying these techniques while actually in the water. Many students still use this technique for learning to swim.

Swimming had finally reached the mainstream public by the arrival of the 20th century. Indoor swimming pools were popping up everywhere. After the Great Depression, the president created several new municipal pools as part of the New Deals Act. Most of the larger towns in America finally had access to public outdoor pools, which allowed more people than ever to start swimming, creating clubs, and competing.

Swimming now ranks second in order of popularity of modern exercises. The great thing is that many of these people don't even realize they are getting great exercise. Swimming is so fun that it doesn't feel like a real workout, but it actually is.

Even in this modern day and age, nearly half of the American population doesn't know how to perform some of the basic swimming techniques or water safety techniques. Water safety and learning swimming techniques, both of which will be covered later in the book, are crucial first steps before beginning a new swimming fitness regime. However, people may not need to know more advanced techniques if they are only interested in leisurely swimming activities.

Swimming for Health

Now that its history is known, it's time to move forward and cover the many health and fitness benefits of swimming. These benefits range from mental benefits, such as stress relief, that can be enjoyed after only ten minutes in the pool, to more long-term benefits, such as improving cardiovascular health and increasing overall muscle endurance.

There's a reason swimming is the second most popular exercise. Aside from the fact that it's really fun, it's also really effective. Swimming works the entire body in a low-impact manner, it teaches proper breathing, and anyone can do it.

Cardio Respiratory Benefits

The term, cardio respiratory, refers to the internal actions of a person's lungs and heart. This is the ability of the circulatory system to deliver blood to the muscles, and the ability of the respiratory system to deliver oxygen to those muscles. The cardio respiratory system is typically mentioned in regards to physical activity and the body's ability to sufficiently fuel itself during these activities.

In general, most forms of exercise are good for the cardio respiratory system. Long-term effects of effective exercises allow the heart muscle to grow and become stronger. This means the heart can pump more blood volume through the body with the same number of beats. Exercise also helps improve the number of smaller arteries that are located inside the muscles.

These exercises improve the respiratory system as well. Regular exercise allows the lungs to inhale more oxygen and deliver it more quickly to the muscles. Any exercise that raises the heart rate and pushes the lungs is likely improving the cardio respiratory system.

Swimming is one of the best exercises out there when it comes to improving the functions and strength of the cardio respiratory system. Swimming actively works most muscles in the body, including the small muscles and the big muscles. Swimming laps is better than most cardiovascular exercises, including jogging, as it usually takes more energy to keep it going for longer periods. Swimming has the best possible impact on the cardio respiratory system when it is performed regularly.

As with most exercises, increasing the speed and intensity of the workout will improve the benefits. Increasing intensity causes the heart to pump harder and faster. It also causes the lungs to work overtime to deliver the necessary oxygen to the muscles. Noticeable improvements become obvious after only a few short months of regular swimming.

A recent study was performed on a group of men and women in their 30s. These men and women took part in swim training courses for a 12-week period. Among those who took the course, max possible oxygen consumption improved 10 percent on average. The stroke volume of the heart, which is the volume of blood that heart bumps per beat, saw an improvement of 18 percent on average.

With scientific research and clinical studies supporting the evidence, it's obvious that swimming is a crucial part of any fitness regime aimed at improving respiratory or cardiovascular function. People at risk for developing heart-related diseases will benefit even more from this new exercise.

Cholesterol

First and foremost, it's important to mention that not all cholesterol is bad for the body. Cholesterol is produced naturally by the body and serves many important functions. It is also obtained by the foods people eat. Cholesterol has a waxy texture, and the majority of the cholesterol needed by the body is produced in the liver. From there, it circulates through the bloodstream.

Many of the foods people eat contain some percentage of cholesterol. The liver also works overtime, producing more cholesterol than usual when eating certain foods. Foods that are high in saturated fats or trans fats will cause the liver to produce more cholesterol.

Over time, too much cholesterol will start to cause havoc inside the body. Leftover cholesterol remains inside the arteries, and this layer of waxy cholesterol makes it much harder for the heart to circulate necessary blood throughout the body.

The plaque inside the arteries may eventually break apart and block passage through them altogether. This may then form a serious blood clot, which reduces the blood reaching the brain and causes a stroke. If the artery that is clotted feeds the heart directly, then the blood clot may lead to a heart attack instead of a stroke.

As mentioned, there is good cholesterol and bad cholesterol inside the body. The "bad" cholesterol is known as LDL cholesterol and the "good" cholesterol is labeled HDL cholesterol. This stands for Low-Density Lipoprotein and High-Density Lipoprotein. These two numbers, when combined with 20 percent of the person's triglyceride level, equals their overall cholesterol count. This number is found via a blood test.

The LDL cholesterol is bad because it leads to the artery plaque and blockage mentioned previously. The clogging of arteries because of LDL is also referred to as atherosclerosis. LDL can also lead to a condition called peripheral artery disease. This occurs when the LDL plaque reduces blood flow to the legs.

HDL, on the other hand, actually helps reduce and remove existing LDL in the body. HDL actually manages to find lingering LDL proteins in the blood stream and then takes that cholesterol back to the liver. Nearly a third of all cholesterol moving through the bloodstream is actually being carried back to the liver by the HDL. Low levels of HDL and high levels of LDL significantly increase the risk for heart attack or stroke.

The best method for reducing LDL and improving HDL is regular exercise. All forms of aerobic and cardiovascular exercise will help lower LDL cholesterol. This includes exercises like walking, running, cycling, and, most importantly, swimming. Swimming is undoubtedly one of the best exercises when it comes to controlling overall cholesterol levels, both LDL and HDL.

Swimming is a great exercise for controlling cholesterol because it pushes the heart rate above 70 percent of its max possible value. Once this 70 percent threshold is crossed for at least 30 minutes a day, significant increases in HDL and decreases in LDL can be observed.

A stunning 33 percent of Americans above the age of 20 suffer from high blood pressure. Nearly half that percentage suffers from high, unsafe levels of bad cholesterol. The percentage is higher amongst women than men.

Swimming at least five times a week is most effective when combined with a sensible diet. Decreasing the amount of trans fat and certain saturated fats is helpful. More than 250,000 people die each year because they fail to get the amount of physical activity required to keep the body healthy. Swimming could make all of the difference between life and death for many people.

Endurance

Muscular endurance is a very important aspect of life, especially for people who are fairly active on a regular basis. Muscle endurance is defined by the formation of slow twitch fibers within the muscle. A slow twitch muscle fiber cannot exert as much force as a fast twitch fiber, but it can easily withstand more effort over a longer duration of time.

Fast twitch muscle fibers, on the other hand, exert larger amounts of force, but for very short periods. Athletes, and people generally concerned about their fitness, put effort into building both fast twitch and slow twitch muscle fibers. Fast twitch fibers result in more strength, and slow twitch fibers result in more muscle endurance.

Muscle endurance is what allows the muscles to continue performing at high levels after they've been in use for more than a few minutes. Most sports depend heavily on an athlete's muscle endurance. After all, if they are out of energy after the first play, then the rest of the game will be a bust. Cross-country, for example, relies purely on endurance and very little on strength.

Muscular endurance is easily improved via cardiovascular exercises, such as swimming. Walking is even a great exercise for building endurance and slow twitch fibers, but it's not nearly as effective as swimming.

Muscle endurance also increases with new capillaries forming within the muscles. These new capillaries allow more oxygen to be delivered to the muscles and muscle fibers. The slow twitch muscle fibers more efficiently use this oxygen as fuel for continuous actions or exercises. Fast twitch fibers rely more on anaerobic metabolism as their fuel source, thus allowing them to create short bursts with high energy levels.

Long distance swimming is a great place to start working on muscle endurance inside the water. Long distance swimming likely has the greatest impact on these slow twitch fibers and cardio respiratory development of new capillaries in these fibers. For developing strength, power, and fast-twitch fibers, swimmers turn to sprint swimming.

Coordination

Many benefits of swimming come from learning proper swimming techniques and maneuvers. Even those who aren't training for competitive swimming still enjoy learning various techniques because many of them present the swimmer with unique benefits.

Most, if not all, proper swimming techniques will improve the swimmer's coordination over time. This is because proper swimming is an art of efficiency and technique. It requires control of the entire body and moving different parts of the body in different directions at the same time. A high level of mental focus is created in such an environment and it can have a noticeable impact on coordination over time.

Swimming is more than just a mental game. Repetitive swimming improves the intermuscular coordination and communication between the brain and the rest of the body. People who learn new swimming techniques or swim new routes on a regular basis experience the opening of new neurological pathways in their brains, which has various beneficial effects on the body, many of which have yet to be deciphered.

Intermuscular coordination can only come from actually swimming. Reading all of the swimming books in the world may prepare a person for the act of swimming, but only getting in the water and swimming the proper techniques time and time again will improve internal coordination efforts.

An improvement in coordination is most definitely a long-term benefit of swimming. First time swimmers may notice no improvement and have a hard time mastering even the simplest techniques. However, like with most other things in life, it is practice that makes perfection.

Arthritis

Swimming is recommended as a physical therapy option for a variety of conditions, illnesses, and symptoms. Arthritis is perhaps one of the most common ailments that benefits tremendously from time spent in the pool.

Exercise is strongly recommended for any patient suffering from arthritis. Time spent in the pool can increase flexibility and strength of the joints, as well as reduce the severity of joint pain. Swimming has a very low-impact on the body, thus making it the ideal exercise for patients with arthritis.

Swimming to combat arthritis also doesn't require the perfect breaststroke. Time spent performing rather leisurely exercises inside a pool will make a big difference. Simply swimming around the pool a few times will reduce symptoms of arthritis and improve joint strength.

Swimming is great for improving joint mobility, which is important, even for people who don't have arthritis. Joint mobility refers to a person's ability to freely move a particular joint. Higher joint mobility is a good thing because it increases the possible range of movement for that joint.

Unlike running or jogging, swimming has another benefit in terms of joint mobility. The repetitive motions required by any proper swimming technique cause joints to increase natural production of synovial fluid. This is the fluid that lubricates the various joints in the body, from knuckle joints to shoulder joints.

Many arthritis patients are under the false pretense that extensive exercise might actually aggravate or increase their symptoms, like pain. In reality, swimming has the exact opposite effect. Swimming builds stronger muscles around the joints, improves bone strength, and even helps lose weight, which reduces pressure on certain joints.

When swimming specifically to deal with arthritis, there are certain exercises that should be performed in the water for the best possible relief. These include range-of-motion, aerobic, and strengthening exercises. Each group has its own particular benefits. Alternating exercises on a schedule is a great technique for squeezing them all in, and it keeps the exercise routine from becoming repetitive.

Aerobic exercises are very important for improving cardiovascular health, which swimming has already been proven to do. In terms of arthritis relief, improved cardiovascular health provides much needed stamina and weight loss. Focusing on weight loss is important for arthritis patients, because extra weight means extra pain.

Twenty to thirty minutes spent swimming at least three times a week is enough to make a difference to the body. Swimming is much easier for arthritis patients than other aerobic exercises.

Range-of-motion exercises are used to improve mobility of the joints. Learn proper swimming techniques with broad, repetitive motions, as they are great for this. These exercises should be performed more frequently than aerobic exercise. Swimming a few laps every day is a great idea.

The final group of exercises is purely for building the muscles that surround the joints. Many gyms have pools with resistance bands and weights available to improve the effectiveness of strength training in the pool. Swimming alone is still enough to improve muscle mass.

Finally, it's important to note that any time spent in the pool can help arthritis sufferers. Even without any notion of an exercise regimen, time spent swimming around the pool and moving the body can still help reduce symptoms. As a matter of fact, nearly any and all movement is a good thing for arthritis patients.

General Physical Therapy

Due to its low-impact nature, swimming is a great form of physical therapy for patients who have recently suffered an injury. This is extremely common in the sports world, where athletes are told they should swim often after an injury to maintain their level of physical fitness.

Swimming demands less of the body, and places less stress on all of the joints and muscles involved. Other forms of exercise may cause pain and discomfort in patients suffering from an injury. Swimming, on the other hand, is very relaxing and causes no additional harm.

The water resists the body as the patient swims in the pool. This resistance means the muscles must work to exert force and move. The water doesn't impact the body. When running, for example, there is a constant and repetitive impact on the body as the feet touch the ground.

Even patients without full use of their legs can get in the water and exercise. A president famously swam frequently despite his polio, which paralyzed his body from the waist down.

Building Muscle Mass

It has been mentioned that swimming is a great exercise for building muscle mass. While swimming alone may not amount to an ideal fitness regime, it is certainly a necessary piece of the overall puzzle. The term "swimmer's body" refers to the toned, muscular form that results from adequate time spent working out in the pool.

Swimming can be classified as a resistance exercise. Most people are already familiar with the term, as many common muscle-building exercises, such as weight lifting, are also classified as resistance exercises.

These are exercises that resist the attempted movement of the body. The muscles must work harder to move against the resistance, thus causing small tears that, when healed, increase the size and strength of the muscles.

However, unlike common resistance exercises like weight lifting, swimming does not place any additional stress on the joints and bones of the body. Nearly every form of weight lifting places some form of stress on the joints, which can lead to serious complications in the future. Swimming places no stress on these joints, thus making it easier to exercise without hurting the body.

Swimming strengthens many of the muscles in the body. Exercises that work all or many of the muscles together are highly recommended, and swimming does exactly that. However, there are some muscles that are favored when swimming. The muscles that will receive the most benefit are the abdominals, legs, and shoulders.

Water resistance comes mostly from the pushing and pulling of the body and limbs through the water. Extended periods of exercise in the water not only improve muscle mass, but also help improve muscle endurance. There are a lot of different exercises that can be incorporated into an underwater environment for improved effects, but simply swimming is the absolute best place to start.

Swimming as a muscle building exercise is accomplished most effectively through the use of main sets. Main sets are just groups of repetitions. The repetitions being repeatedly swimming a certain distance, typically 100 yards. Most swimmers perform a set of at least eight 100-yard repetitions.

As with most other workouts, the body and muscles eventually get used to the resistance of the water. To continue improving strength, the swimmer must increase the length of their sets or the number of repetitions. This is the best and safest method for increasing the intensity of swimming. Increasing intensity is necessary as the swimmer becomes stronger.

The Mental Aspect

There are a lot of people who are eager to lose weight, gain muscle, and get healthy, but they just can't seem to follow through. Many times, they simply get bored of repetitive workout sessions. Once they get bored with the exercises, it gets easier to push them to the side and eventually forget them altogether.

Swimming is great because it allows such a wide variety of exercises. It's impossible to get bored with swimming, especially considering that many people swim just for fun and without any intention of getting fit.

Simple variations in the length of the sets can make a big difference. Swimmers like to mix things up, choosing something like two sets of 100-yard sprints one day, and more 50-yard sets the following day. Changing intervals and timing keeps the body surprised and prevents it from becoming too relaxed or too bored.

Swimming requires extensive control of the mind and body, which requires serious focus. Focusing on swimming itself helps distract the mind from fatigue. This is also one of the reasons why swimming is such a great tool for fighting stress.

Stress

Stress is a serious problem that millions of people deal with on a daily basis. A century ago, stress was believed to be little more than an attitude problem. Today, it's recognized as a leading factor in many mental and physical conditions.

In a general sense, stress includes any time that a person feels under pressure. A stressor is any stimulus that induces pressure or stress on an individual. Most people have their own unique stressors, while they also share many stressors in common. Noises, events, and even other people could become a potential stressor to a particular individual.

In many cases, whether the person realizes it or not, the body immediately responds to stress with a fight or flight response. This is a serious response that occurs on many levels: mental, physical, and biological. Heart rate increases, the body produces more cortisol, and adrenaline increases depending on the degree and nature of the stress.

There are other significant changes in the body during a moment of stress. Blood pressure increases, and the immune system actually stops working. The rate of breathing increases, along with an increase in heart rate. The digestive system begins working more slowly, and muscles throughout the body become tense. These are all symptoms and signs of noticeable stress.

A study has shown that a person's perception of stress actually impacts their stress and has physical repercussions. The same study showed that people who believed their stress was hurting their health were actually 100 percent more likely to have a heart attack within the next ten years. A subjective perception of stress plays a big role in the eventual outcome.

The use of swimming to reduce stress dates back nearly as long as swimming itself. Almost everyone who gets in the water can agree that it is an enjoyable and relaxing experience. This alone is enough to help reduce stress levels in even the toughest situation.

Furthermore, the act of swimming, particularly when using proper techniques, requires full dedication of the mind. The act of focusing purely on swimming frees the mind from all other stressors in the world. It's very easy to get lost in a half hour of doing the breaststroke and forget all about that job promotion, ex-wife, and upcoming business deal.

Meditation is often advised as a method for dealing with stress in the short and long term. There are many, many different forms of meditation, and it's all about finding what is comfortable and works for the patient.

Most people are familiar with sitting meditation, which is where the individual sits still, usually in a cross-legged position, and finds their internal peace. However, not everyone is familiar with moving mediation, which is a great way to mix it up a bit and possibly find an entirely new state of mind.

Many modern professionals are recommending swimming as a form of relaxing, moving meditation. It's almost as if swimming was designed with this purpose in mind. The movements, the thought process, even the gentle sounds of water all work together to create this ideal environment for reaching a state of Zen and relieving stress.

Here are a couple of tips for turning an evening of swimming into a form of moving meditation.

1. Reduce the speed.

Swimming to meditate and swimming to get fit are two very different things. Many people who already use swimming as a form of meditation have stated that finding the perfect speed is a key first step towards achieving peace. That means ignoring the clocks, the times, the speeds, and simply slowing down.

Stressful gulps of air are common amongst inexperienced swimmers. First and foremost, learning to swim properly and spending time in the pool will slowly remove these anxious feeling and habits. From there, learning proper breathing techniques, similar to those used during yoga, will help reduce the urge to increase speed, thus maintaining a peaceful state.

2. Get in a rhythm.

Finding a rhythm is very important to many forms of meditation, particularly when breathing. One's breathing rhythm is something that is used as a center of focus to clear their mind. Learning to breath in rhythm is often more difficult than actually breathing in rhythm. In due time, it will simply become second nature to the swimmer.

The particular breathing rhythm will also depend on the swimming technique used. The breaststroke is a very good example of a swimming method that allows for optimum breathing patterns.

3. Use the nose.

Breathing through the nose is very important, in terms of meditation and general health. Nose breathing is believed to be the proper breathing technique for all situations. The nose can properly regulate the air that enters the lungs, while breathing through the mouth is very unpredictable, at least from the lungs' point of view.

Slowly exhaling through the nose accomplishes a few things. First, it helps slow down the entire breathing process. As mentioned in the first step, slowing things down is a crucial part of the moving meditation process. Furthermore, it can also create a nice stream of bubbles in the water. How could a stream of bubbles be important?

4. Find something to focus on.

The final tip for moving meditation is finding something in the pool to focus on and clear the mind. For some folks, it's very easy to focus on the sound and rhythm of their breathing, especially if they've already performed forms of meditation out of the water.

If breathing isn't enough, then another favorite amongst swimming meditators is focusing on the stream of bubbles that are created when exhaling slowly through the nostrils beneath the water line. There are plenty of other visual and auditory stimuli in most pools.

Safety When Swimming

Whether at the beach, an Olympic swimming pool, or in an 18th century bathhouse, safety should always be the number one priority in the water. Several thousand people drown every year in America alone. Drowning is one of the top leading accidental causes of death in children between the ages of 1 and 19. The vast majority of these accidents occur at home pools.

In most cases, drowning could have been avoided by learning some fairly basic swimming safety rules.

Actually Learn to Swim

It might sound obvious, but unfortunately a lot of drowning deaths occur because people who can't swim get in over their head without anyone else around to help. Learning to swim is the necessary, yet often overlooked, first step towards actually swimming to improve health and fitness.

Luckily, many of those ideals from centuries ago are appearing once again in modern culture. Certain organizations and schools are more than willing to teach today's youth how to swim and how to stay safe in the water. Until then, it's all shallow waters and nearby lifeguards.

Free-swimming lessons are a great idea for the kids, but what about the adults? There are plenty of swimming classes and courses designed specifically for adults; however, most of these courses are not free for adults.

The YMCA is a great example of an organization that regularly hosts swimming classes. Their classes range from a beginner's course, to more advanced classes that teach specific strokes and even synchronized swimming skills. Advanced courses at the YMCA also cover some diving skills.

However, it's that beginner's course that is the most important. The beginner's course teaches the basic fundamentals of personal safety while around or in the water. These skills include accident prevention, self-rescue, and needed survival skills. All of these are necessary to enjoy indoor and outdoor swimming safely.

Beginner's courses also focus on teaching some of the basic stroke techniques. Students should learn to tread water, paddle, and possibly even learn the basics of breaststroke. They'll also learn some basic rescue skills while swimming, in case they ever need to save someone else in the water.

Finally, no course is complete without a little fun. The YMCA is known for incorporating engaging water games into their classes. It's an overall enjoyable and useful experience.

Don't Let Children Swim Alone

This next safety tip is geared more towards helping children. Drowning doesn't require much water. As a matter of fact, drowning can take place in as little as two inches of water. Studies also show that the highest percentage of accidental drowning happens with children between the ages of 1 and 4 and at their home.

The problem here is often that the child is left unsupervised in the pool. Leaving the poolside for as little as five minutes can pose a potential hazard to a child's life. All professionals agree that children should never be left unsupervised in the water, whether at a swimming pool at home or at the beach.

Parents with a pool at home are advised to install a fence around the pool area. The fence should be at least four feet tall. It's there to separate the pool and concrete from the rest of the home or the rest of yard. A self-latching gate keeps the area safe and prevents children from entering when there aren't any adults present at the pool.

Wait for the Lifeguard

Lifeguards are usually trained, certified individuals who understand water safety, rules, and rescue. Anytime a person is swimming in a non-residential pool, it's always recommended that they make sure a lifeguard is present. Even if they know how to swim, it's still a good idea to have an active lifeguard present just in case there is an unforeseen accident. It's even more important for people who can't swim.

All public swimming pools have their own rules and regulations. A lot of these rules are similar and are there for the safety of the swimmers. Swimmers, even experienced swimmers, must follow these rules and the directions of the lifeguard at all times.

The presence of a lifeguard still isn't a good reason to leave a child unsupervised. It's not the lifeguard's job to babysit, and it's likely not allowed at most public swimming pools.

Drugs and Alcohol

Everyone is allowed their own opinions concerning drugs and alcohol, but one thing is always true, they don't mix with swimming. The influence of any such substance significantly impairs coordination and judgment skills, which are both entirely necessary for safe and proper swimming.

This is obviously not allowed at public swimming areas, but it's recommended to follow this advice even when swimming in a personal pool at home. The risk for serious injury, and even death, increases significantly when drugs or alcohol are added to the occasion.

One drink is too many before jumping in the pool. Remember, it only takes two inches of water for a person to drown. Slipping or falling because of intoxication could result in drowning, especially if someone else isn't present, as they should be.

There are plenty of other rules that are commonplace in public swimming areas, but obviously can't be enforced at home. However, all of these rules are there for safety reasons, thus they should be adhered to at home by safety-conscious swimmers who want to reduce their risk of injury.

Horseplay is another great example of public swimming regulation with a reason. It's so much fun to be in a pool that it's easy to quickly get carried away dunking, hanging, or throwing people in the water. This seriously increases the risk for injury or drowning, especially with swimmers who aren't as experienced. There are plenty of safe, fun activities to do in the water that pose a much smaller risk to the swimmer.

Diving headfirst into the pool is also something that should be avoided. Diving into shallow water headfirst can result in severe head injuries. If there isn't a lifeguard present, then it could lead to death. It's easiest to just avoid diving headfirst into any water, period. Instead, always jump in feet first, and always know the depth of the water beforehand.

Swimmers should never be in the water during a thunderstorm. Swimming pools are closed during these times because a swimming pool is a great conductor of electricity. Water is a much better conductor than air, and presents far less resistance to electrical current.

Accidents have happened in pools, and even outdoors at public beaches, where a single lightning strike severely injures multiple swimmers. Lifeguards should present swimmers with clear and concise instructions for safely exiting the pool anytime thunder is heard. No health benefits are worth being struck by lightning.

Cardiopulmonary Resuscitation (CPR)

It's advised for any swimmers or parents of children who swim to take a course and learn some proper first aid and CPR techniques. Knowing these crucial, life-saving skills could make all of the difference if an accident should unfortunately occur in the water. CPR isn't a very complicated process, but if performed correctly, it can save lives.

CPR is actually used for a variety of different emergencies. Learning CPR can benefit swimmers outside of the pool as well. In general it's just a good thing to know. CPR is also extremely helpful for victims having a heart attack.

Those who aren't trained with proper CPR techniques can still do their part to save the life of a drowning person. Doing something is always better than waiting and doing nothing at all. Untrained individuals are advised to perform hands-only CPR.

Hands-only CPR refers only to repetitive compressions of the chest using the palms. This should occur at a rate of around 100 compressions per minute. It's continued until the paramedics arrive on the scene, or the individual regains consciousness. Untrained professionals aren't advised to attempt rescue breathing, otherwise known as "mouth-to-mouth resuscitation".

Those who have taken a course, as they should, and are confident in their ability to perform, should be aware that CPR is more likely to be successful when sets of chest compressions are paired with rescue breathing and checking the airways.

The great thing about CPR is that can be used on just about everyone, excluding newborn babies. That includes adults, seniors, and infants alike. Even if the person doesn't return to consciousness, the CPR will keep blood and oxygen moving throughout the body, thus preventing brain damage, which occurs within 10 minutes of oxygen deprivation.

Swimming Techniques

Whether or not you're aiming to become a professional swimmer, learning proper swimming techniques makes a big difference in the water. Also referred to as "stroke techniques" these are the methods used to move around the water without sinking to the bottom. They require use of the head, torso, arms, and legs. The placement of the head often determines the appropriate breathing technique for the stroke.

Front Crawl

Freestyle competitions are swimming events where swimmers can choose from just about any personal swimming style they prefer. Despite the freedom, almost every swimmer chooses to use the front crawl or some variation of this crawl. Many people are referring specifically to the front crawl when they talk about freestyle swimming.

The front crawl is the primary freestyle swimming technique, because it is believed to be the fastest of all the stroke techniques. The front crawl is one of two official long axis strokes, along with backstroke. Front crawl strokes are not regulated by the FINA, but most swimmers will stick to a fairly similar methodology.

The front crawl is performed in a facedown position in the water, which allows for a larger range of motion than backstroke. The strokes of the arm go below water and then recover above the water, which creates a noticeable reduction in drag. In comparison, breaststrokes recover underwater, which places more resistance and drag on the arm, thus reducing speed.

Swimmers will alternate arm strokes and roll the body at the same time. The rolling movement improves breathing rhythm and allows for an easier recovery of the stroking arm. The alternating motion also allows for a consistent speed throughout all of the swimming cycle.

The front crawl has been around for thousands of years. The Egyptian paintings mentioned earlier in the book were believed to depict ancients performing the front crawl. The front crawl became more popular in 1844, when a Native American used it at a London swimming competition to defeat a local swimmer who used breaststroke.

Even with that victory, the British people refused to use the front crawl. They believed it was a barbaric method for swimming and caused too much water to splash around. It was considered very un-European. It didn't return again until after 1873, when it was learned in South America by John Trudgen and performed in a swimming competition held in Great Britain.

The modern front crawl variation used most often today is a take from the "American Crawl". Charles Daniels created the American Crawl. It takes the traditional six-beat kick and makes slight modifications. It's extremely effective, fast, and works equally well over short and long distances.

The breathing cycle and rhythm for any stroke technique is very important. With the modern front crawl, swimmers breathe once every third time an arm recovers, or returns to the forward position. This would be one breath every one and a half cycles. Experienced competitors increase this number to one breath every second stroke, which equates to one breath per cycle.

Breaststroke

Breaststroke is similar to the front crawl in some regards. The swimmer is placed on their chest and swims in a forward motion using a combination of the arms and legs, but there is no rotation of the torso or head. While front crawl is believed to be the fastest stroke, breaststroke is the most popular amongst recreational swimmers who swim for fun, exercise, or health.

Most swimmers learn breaststroke as their first swimming technique. Breaststroke is so popular recreationally because it's easy to learn and it allows the swimmer to keep their heads above the water for the majority of the cycle. It's also possible to comfortably perform breaststroke at slower speeds than other methods.

Once at a competitive level, performing breaststroke becomes far more difficult. The difficulty comes from large amounts of energy and oxygen it takes to perform this stroke technique at high speeds. Other strokes consume much less energy and are easier to sustain for longer periods of time. Breaststroke is also called the "frog stroke" at times, because the movements of the swimmer greatly resemble a frog in the water.

For the reasons listed above, breaststroke is actually the slowest of all four-stroke variations officially recognized by the FINA. On record, the fastest breaststroke swimmer averages around 1.5 meters per second performing this stroke. Not only is it the slowest, but it's also one of the most difficult to perform properly. Regardless, it is still extremely popular.

The basics of the stroke are pretty easy to grasp. The swimmer takes a position leaning forward with the arms only slightly breaking the surface of the water. The legs always remain underwater. The head breaks beneath the water only once per cycle, during the second half.

The angle of movement poses a serious problem in terms of speed. The body is at such a steep angle compared to other methods that it slows the swimmer down and requires more energy to move faster. Professionals who prefer the use of breaststroke must focus on building strong abdominal muscles for adding additional power to the "frog kick" or "whip-kick" of each cycle.

There are some odd regulations concerning breaststroke for those who are swimming in a competitive fashion. For example, swimmers are allowed to perform something known as the dolphin kick, but only once as the arms are moving down. This is slightly more advanced than anything the average, recreational swimmer needs to use for fitness.

Breaststroke is a great swimming technique for exercise, relaxation, and meditation. It's easier to perform at slower speeds, making it ideal for people who want to spend some leisurely time in the pool, but enjoy a bit of a workout at the same time.

The motions of breaststroke are a great point of focus for people interested in moving meditation while swimming. Many agree it is the best stroke for such things.

Backstroke

The second long-axis stroke, after the front crawl, is backstroke. It is also one of the four styles recognized by the FINA, and it is the only swimming style that is performed entirely on the back. Swimming on the back allows the swimmer to breathe much easier, but it prevents them from actually seeing where they are swimming.

Backstroke shares similarities with front crawl and butterfly. In terms of speed, it is closest to butterfly. The fastest being front crawl and the slowest being breaststroke. On average, swimmers can cross about 1.8 meters per second using backstroke.

When performing backstroke in a competitive setting, the swimmers must start from a different position than when using any of the other three techniques. This causes backstroke to have slower times than butterfly. However, when swum consistently for 200 meters, it is backstroke that often proves to be faster. It is still largely dependent on the swimmer's stamina levels.

Unlike other techniques, backstroke relies on more upper-body muscles than core muscles. The difference in muscles worked means that swimmers can use backstroke and breaststroke during alternating sets to work more muscles in the body than usual. This improves flexibility, mobility, and helps build muscle more effectively.

Butterfly

The final stroke technique covered by the FINA is butterfly. This is a complex technique that is swum from the chest and requires both arms to move in unison. At the same time as the arms are moving, the swimmer must also perform the butterfly kick, which is also known as the dolphin kick. The dolphin kick was later incorporated into breaststroke.

Most beginners shy away from learning butterfly. It is likely the most difficult style to master because of its reliance on strong muscles, perfect movement, and difficult technique. Butterfly is also the newest swimming style to be swum in competitive form and most recently to be recognized by the FINA. It was first introduced during the 1930's.

Butterfly actually has a top speed that surpasses that of front crawl. However, front crawl faces less resistance during the recovery, which allows for much better times over the long run. Speeds drop drastically during the recovery phase of butterfly because so much of the body is under water at one time.

Other techniques, such as front crawl and backstroke, can still be swum if the swimmer's technique isn't perfect. Butterfly, on the other hand, requires near flawless execution or it won't work at all. A poor butterfly technique is slow, ineffective, and likely won't keep the swimmer afloat.

The primary problem when it comes to learning butterfly is mastering the unified recovery of the entire body during each cycle. The chest, head, arms, and shoulders must all move together and recover together, while the swimmer is managing a proper breathing cycle.

It can be extremely difficult and tedious for new swimmers to learn butterfly, let alone race competitively. It is definitely a technique more suited towards the professional or swimmer with a lot of experience already under their belt.

The creation of the butterfly stroke is credited to Sydney Cavill from Australia. His father, Frederick, was regarded as the "Professor of Swimming". Sydney was the Australian champion of the 220-yard amateurs at the age of only 16. He would later come to America and coach many of the great swimmers who would later compete in the Olympics.

Henry Myers at the YMCA swam the butterfly stroke in competition in 1933. This stroke evolved from a variation of the more-common breaststroke. The name doesn't come from the butterfly kick, but rather the butterfly movement of the arms coming over the water in front of the body.

Swimming for Health and Fitness: In Summary

At the end of the day, there's no denying what a powerful, effective, and enjoyable workout swimming provides. In a world where people deny their fitness needs because they simply aren't "fun enough", it's good to know there is an activity already perceived as fun that's also extremely healthy.

What Makes Swimming So Great?

Swimming is a low-impact exercise. When a person is getting regular exercise outdoors, there is almost always some form of impact on the body. Running, jogging, and many other standing exercises create a ground impact on the body. This occurs as the body regains contact with the ground and force is transferred between the two.

There's absolutely no ground impact when swimming. As a matter of fact, there's rarely contact with solids of any sort when swimming. The lack of ground impact makes swimming an excellent exercise for people with conditions such as arthritis, inflammation, or weak bones.

After a day spent exercising in the pool, the only part of the body that might hurt is the muscles, and that's only because they got such a good workout in the pool. The Arthritis Foundation is so confident of the benefits of swimming for arthritis patients that they regularly sponsor swimming courses all throughout the country.

Swimming alone isn't the only great exercise in the pool. Water aerobics encompasses an entire niche of exercises and workout routines that focus on improving the body via the resistance of water. Using flotation devices during water aerobics lessens the likelihood of touching the bottom of the pool and taking slight ground impact.

Because there is so little impact when swimming, it's an exercise that a person can perform basically their entire lives. When seniors aren't able to lift weights or run for miles, they can still get in the pool and maintain a healthy, active lifestyle. Look at nearly any swimming competition and you'll find age groups that accommodate people between 100 and 104 years old! Jack La Lanne was a fitness expert who swam every day for at least one hour until the age of 93.

Of course, something just being easy doesn't make it great. Swimming is great because it works wonders for improving the cardiovascular and respiratory systems within the body. Countless studies have been performed over the centuries, and all of them point to swimming as having a positive impact on blood flow and oxygen consumption.

For those who want to lose weight, swimming has become that fun, enjoyable exercise they have been waiting for. Swimming doesn't burn quite as many calories as running with high intensity, but it burns about 89 percent of the same amount. Considering how much more enjoyable swimming is compared to running, many agree it's a worthy trade.

Swimming may burn as many as 650 calories an hour during a high-intensity workout. Oddly enough, swimmers actually burn more calories by randomly flopping arms and legs around in the water than using any of the mentioned swimming techniques.

A person's body weight and body mass index (BMI) impacts their buoyancy, which also determines how many calories they can burn while swimming. People with more body fat burn fewer calories because they are naturally more buoyant than the average person.

It's important to realize that calorie burning is heavily dependent on the intensity of the exercise. A person swimming may burn more calories than when running for the same period of time, but only if the intensity of the swimming is higher. Swimming at average speeds burns more calories than low-intensity running or walking.

Burning calories and losing weight isn't enough for most people. Building new muscle mass is a big part of fitness, and swimming helps accomplish this task as well. Another study was performed on men who took a swimming program for a full eight weeks. The study revealed there was an average increase of 23 percent of the triceps.

Many people worry that swimming may not be as intense as their current workout routine, thus it couldn't possibly help build new muscle mass. That is the case sometimes, but can be remedied by swimming faster for longer periods of time. Adding new aquatic aerobics to the mix can help as well. Even with existing muscle mass, swimming regularly helps tone the body in a way that no other exercise can do.

Muscle mass is very important, but so is muscle endurance. Muscle endurance comes from forming new capillaries in the muscles and creating new slow-twitch muscle fibers. Both of these things will come with a regular swimming fitness regime.

Another one of the many great aspects of swimming is that it can be a very social activity. People are more eager to get up and exercise when they know they aren't doing it alone. Swimming programs offer new and experienced swimmers a chance to meet with others who are doing the same thing and possibly trying to reach similar goals.

It's also a great activity for the entire family. It's difficult to convince a young child that they should be doing push-ups, but mention the pool and they'll be packed, in the car, and ready to go within five minutes. Swimming can help fight obesity, which can be a genetic condition, by encouraging the whole family to get out and exercise together.

Finally, there's just nothing out there that's quite as fun and refreshing as jumping in a cool pool during the hot summer months. Strenuous exercise is made even more difficult during the summer heat. The heat may even pose a potential health risk to people with certain medical conditions.

Swimming offers these people the chance they need to get the exercise they require during the summer without putting themselves at any risk. At the same time, they enjoy a relaxing experience, possibly with friends and family.

The Various Swimming Strokes

Swimming has a lot of uses, whether it's just for fun, for hobby, for meditation, for exercise, or for sport. All of these uses have something in common: they require some form of stroke technique to actually move around the water. People have developed, invented, modified, and reinvented many different techniques over the years, but there are four which are still used primarily today.

In terms of recreational use, breaststroke is the most common swimming technique used today. It's very easy to maintain a constant low-speed while performing breaststroke. Most people don't perform breaststroke perfectly, as it's much more difficult to do on a competitive level.

In terms of exercise, a slow, reliable stroke technique is exactly what the swimmer needs. In terms of competitive racing, breaststroke is the slowest and least favored of the entire stroke techniques. It becomes more difficult to maintain at higher speeds without wasting energy.

Breaststroke is also very common because of its breathing patterns. The neck is not rotated during the cycle, which allows for consistent breathing without repetitively gasping for air while rotating the neck. Swimmers only submerge their head once during each cycle.

Front crawl is on the opposite end of the spectrum. This is the fastest overall stroke technique. People often refer to freestyle and front crawl as the same thing. Freestyle is a race where the swimmer can use any swimming technique they prefer, but they almost always use front crawl because of its faster speed.

Backstroke is the only official stroke technique performed on the back. It, perhaps, allows the best possible breathing pattern, but has one obvious flaw: the swimmer has no idea where they are going.

In terms of recreation and exercise, backstroke is the second most helpful technique. Most people combine the two techniques, backstroke and breaststroke, because they both work different groups of muscles in the body. Getting a full-body workout is always a good idea, thus creating an exercise regimen that involves both styles would be the most effective.

The final and newest stroke technique is the butterfly. It's the most difficult technique to learn and not something really performed in a recreational sense. The other techniques are more than enough to get in the water and get fit.

It doesn't take a complex stroke technique, an Olympic size swimming pool, or a book from the 18th century to appreciate the many health and fitness benefits of swimming. Getting in the water and moving around is more than enough to get started with swimming fitness.

15064315R00027

Printed in Great Britain
by Amazon.co.uk, Ltd.,
Marston Gate.